# INVASIVE SPECIES
# NUTRIA

by Alicia Z. Klepeis

POGO

# Ideas for Parents and Teachers

Pogo Books let children practice reading informational text while introducing them to nonfiction features such as headings, labels, sidebars, maps, and diagrams, as well as a table of contents, glossary, and index.

Carefully leveled text with a strong photo match offers early fluent readers the support they need to succeed.

## Before Reading

- "Walk" through the book and point out the various nonfiction features. Ask the student what purpose each feature serves.
- Look at the glossary together. Read and discuss the words.

## Read the Book

- Have the child read the book independently.
- Invite him or her to list questions that arise from reading.

## After Reading

- Discuss the child's questions. Talk about how he or she might find answers to those questions.
- Prompt the child to think more. Ask: Nutria spend a lot of time in water. Can you name any other animals that spend much of their lives in water?

Pogo Books are published by Jump!
5357 Penn Avenue South
Minneapolis, MN 55419
www.jumplibrary.com

Library of Congress Cataloging-in-Publication Data

Names: Klepeis, Alicia, 1971– author.
Title: Nutria / by Alicia Z. Klepeis.
Description: Minneapolis, MN: Jump!, Inc., [2023] | Series: Invasive species | Includes index.
Audience: Ages 7–10
Identifiers: LCCN 2022005166 (print)
LCCN 2022005167 (ebook)
ISBN 9781636908014 (hardcover)
ISBN 9781636908021 (paperback)
ISBN 9781636908038 (ebook)
Subjects: LCSH: Coypu–Juvenile literature.
Introduced mammals–Juvenile literature.
Classification: LCC QL737.R668 K54 2023 (print)
LCC QL737.R668 (ebook) | DDC 599.35/9–dc23/
eng/20220208
LC record available at https://lccn.loc.gov/2022005166
LC ebook record available at https://lccn.loc.gov/2022005167

Editor: Eliza Leahy
Designer: Michelle Sonnek

Photo Credits: Eric Isselee/Shutterstock, cover; Voren1/iStock, 1; photomaster/Shutterstock, 3; Oleksandr Lytvynenko/Shutterstock, 4; SannePhoto/Shutterstock, 5; UbjsP/Shutterstock, 6-7; Igor Normann/Shutterstock, 8 (left); Karol Kozlowski/Shutterstock, 8 (right); GarysFRP/iStock, 9; JakubD/Shutterstock, 10-11; Paul Reeves Photography/Shutterstock, 12-13 (top); Paul Nicholson/Shutterstock, 12-13 (bottom); Buiten-Beeld/Alamy, 14-15; Geoff Eccles/iStock, 16-17; Nature Picture Library/SuperStock, 18; Mikhail Varentsov/Shutterstock, 19; jaimie tuchman/Shutterstock, 20-21; Litvalifa/Shutterstock, 23.

Printed in the United States of America at Corporate Graphics in North Mankato, Minnesota.

# TABLE OF CONTENTS

# CHAPTER 1

## SUPER SWIMMERS

What **aquatic** animal has a long tail and big, orange teeth? It is a nutria! This **mammal** spends a lot of time in water. But its body is covered in fur.

**webbing**

A nutria has strong back legs. It has **webbing** between its back toes. This helps it paddle through the water. It is a super swimmer!

Nutria are **native** to South America. Many live in **wetlands** and rivers. But nutria can also live in cities. Some live in storm drains. Others live on golf courses.

Nutria often dig **burrows** to live in. They use their big teeth and strong feet to build them.

## DID YOU KNOW?

Nutria can be more than two feet (0.6 meters) long. They can weigh more than 20 pounds (9.1 kilograms). They look similar to beavers. But beavers are bigger.

burrow

# CHAPTER 2

## RUINING WETLANDS

Today, nutria live on every **continent** except Antarctica and Australia. They are an **invasive species** in many places. People brought them to new areas. Why? Nutria fur is thick and soft. People make it into clothing.

fur boots

fur hat

wetland

Nutria arrived in the United States by the early 1900s. By the mid-1900s, people were buying less fur. Some people set nutria free into the wild. Other nutria escaped. Many made their homes in rivers and wetlands.

Nutria spread quickly. How? They produce a lot of young. An adult female can have three **litters** each year. Some litters have up to 13 babies!

# TAKE A LOOK!

Where do nutria live in the United States? Take a look!

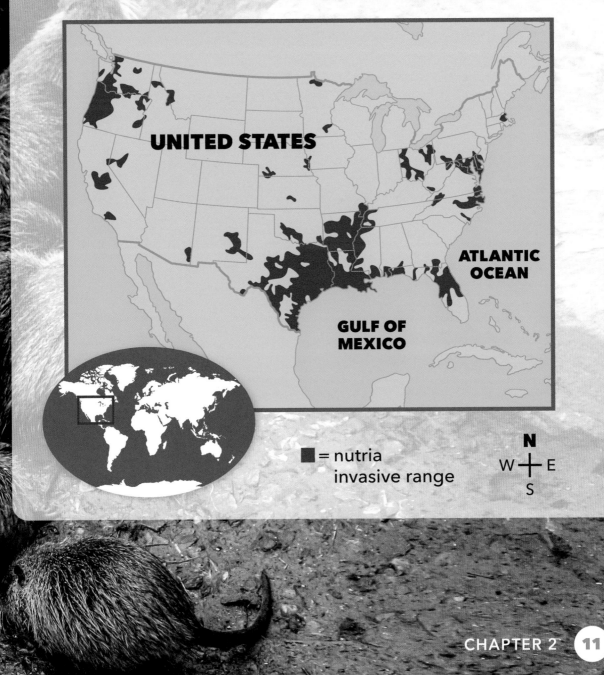

UNITED STATES

ATLANTIC OCEAN

GULF OF MEXICO

■ = nutria invasive range

N
W—E
S

muskrat

trumpeter swan

Nutria eat a lot. They mainly eat aquatic plants. But unlike many other animals, they eat the entire plant. This causes big problems. Why? The plants may not grow back. This takes food away from native animals. Animals such as muskrats and trumpeter swans have less to eat.

## DID YOU KNOW?

Nutria eat about 25 percent of their weight in food each day. That would be like an 8-year-old eating 15 pounds (6.8 kg) of food each day!

25%

Fewer wetland plants can mean more **erosion**. The plants nutria eat help hold soil together. With fewer plants, soil can wash away. Burrows can also cause erosion. A wetland can turn into open water. This can lead to flooding. It also takes **habitat** away from native animals.

erosion

levee

Nutria cause problems for humans, too. Nutria dig burrows under roads, bridges, and buildings. This weakens these structures. **Levees** can break. This can cause flooding.

**DID YOU KNOW?**

Nutria eat **crops**. They damage gardens and lawns, too.

# CHAPTER 3

## TRACK AND TRAP

Many people are working to remove nutria from the United States. Scientists **track** and trap them. Then, the nutria are **euthanized**.

trap

fence ◀ ·····

People put up fences. These can help keep nutria out. Some fences are partly underground. This can stop nutria from digging burrows.

Wetlands in the United States would be healthier without nutria. Native animals would be healthier, too.

You can help native wildlife. How? Grow native plants. Learn about wetland animals near you. The wildlife will thank you!

# ACTIVITIES & TOOLS

## MAKE A WETLAND DIORAMA

Wetlands are home to many animals. Make a wetland diorama in this activity!

**What You Need:**

- books, magazines, or a computer
- sheets of paper
- glue
- a shoebox or other small box
- crayons, colored pencils, or markers
- modeling clay, plants, and/or found objects

❶ Use books, magazines, or a computer to learn about wetlands in your area. Choose one.

❷ Research what kinds of plants and animals live there.

❸ On a sheet of paper, draw a background scene. It should look similar to photos you have seen of your local wetland. Glue it to the inside of the shoebox.

❹ Find plants outside or make some out of paper or clay. Add them to your diorama.

❺ Create native wetland animals out of paper or clay. Place them in your diorama.

❻ Add plants, animals, and other habitat features until you are happy with how your wetland diorama looks. What do you think this wetland would look like if nutria moved in?

# GLOSSARY

**aquatic:** Living in or often found in water.

**burrows:** Tunnels or holes in the ground that some animals make and live in.

**continent:** One of the seven large landmasses on Earth.

**crops:** Plants that are grown as food.

**erosion:** The wearing away of something by water or wind.

**euthanized:** Put to death in a humane manner.

**habitat:** A place where an animal or plant is usually found.

**invasive species:** Any kind of living organism that is not native to a specific area.

**levees:** Banks built near rivers to prevent flooding.

**litters:** Groups of baby animals that are born at the same time to one animal.

**mammal:** A warm-blooded animal that has hair or fur and usually gives birth to live babies.

**native:** Growing or living naturally in a particular area of the world.

**track:** To follow and try to find an animal by looking for marks or traces of it.

**webbing:** Folds of skin that connect toes.

**wetlands:** Areas of land where there is a lot of moisture in the soil.

## INDEX

## TO LEARN MORE

Finding more information is as easy as 1, 2, 3.

❶ Go to www.factsurfer.com

❷ Enter "nutria" into the search box.

❸ Choose your book to see a list of websites.

**FACT SURFER**